Eigenheim

Eigenheim

poetry by
Joanne Epp

TURNSTONE PRESS

Turnstone Press
Artspace Building
206-100 Arthur Street
Winnipeg, MB
R3B 1H3 Canada
www.TurnstonePress.com

Turnstone Press gratefully acknowledges the assistance of the Canada´ Council for the Arts, the Manitoba Arts Council, the Government of Canada through the Canada Book Fund, and the Province of Manitoba through the Book Publishing Tax Credit and the Book Publisher Marketing Assistance Program.

Printed and bound in Canada by Friesens for Turnstone Press.

Library and Archives Canada Cataloguing in Publication

Epp, Joanne, 1963-, author

    Eigenheim : poetry / by Joanne Epp.

Poems.

ISBN 978-0-88801-517-4 (pbk.)

    I. Title.

PS8609.P65E54 2015   C811'.6   C2014-907889-7

Contents

Eigenheim, das (n.): one's own home

eigen (adj.): own; separate
characteristic
peculiar

Eigenheim is a place of which we know the centre,
but not the circumference.
—Walter Klaassen

Eigenheim

Catherine

How dear to her is the journey of the mind,
flying from dwelling to dwelling

—Anne Szumigalski

Names

Catherine under the old pine dreaming
dreams herself small and feather-light.
She climbs the old pine and sways
at the top, taking a branch
to brush her hair from her eyes
before letting go—or is it the branch
that shakes her free? She floats
across the pine-tops, calls each one by name,
then drifts on a passing downdraft
to join the rows of stones
and names on stones.

She knows they are nothing: no bones,
no blood, only voices thin and shimmering
as spiderwebs. She knows how easily
they disperse, like dandelion fluff,
like feathers in the wind.
Their names are all that holds them here.

What are you?

Catherine knows a woman in a small house
in the midst of a tangled garden.
The woman sits in a rocking chair,
holes in her slippers, sweater buttons askew.
Children come to steal apples
and peep through her windows.
Sometimes when the door's ajar
they come inside, feeling reckless and bold.
Catherine follows them.

The woman leans forward, startling them:
I'll tell you something—I was once a cat.
I slept all day, and at night
I went where no one could follow me.
Then I was a wolf. When I spoke
on moonlit nights, folks shivered in their beds
though I never touched a hair of 'em.
And I was once a Night Mare, with a secret nest
lined with feathers and bones. I ran so swiftly
no one could see me except in their dreams.

Now—tell me, what are you?
They stare, dig their toes into the rug.
One of them whispers.

The children drift toward the door.
Catherine watches. When she turns
the woman is still rocking, looking at her.
Catherine looks back, not moving.
They listen to the flies bang the window screens,
each waiting for the other to speak.

Passage

Catherine, walking at night, thinks of what lies
outside the reach of streetlamps. What light makes
invisible. Whose breath she almost hears
at the mouth of an alley. If she turns
her back she might perceive a movement
in her direction, a gaze fixed on her outline.
She's tempted to defy all warnings, leave
the lighted sidewalk for a dark passage.
Once, she walked alone among poplars
on a moonless night, discerning the terrain
with small steps, her eyes hard-pressed
to judge depth or nearness. The night
a solid thing that would still let her fall.
She remembers fear, but longs to go back
to that place where nothing happened, where
she could mistake her luck for courage.
Here in the lane behind the café, she might
be lucky, or she might not. This frightens her
less than it should. Less than slipping below
the surface of her thought, sifting through
its drifted leaves.

Coming home

This much is certain: it was her house,
her cat, her mess left in the kitchen.
It was her name written in red
on the note tacked to the front door.

But the shock when she stepped in:
strangers at her table, drinking her coffee.
Talking about new cabinets, laughing
at her mismatched plates and green fridge.

They turned toward her, shameless,
unsurprised. Expecting her to see
they knew best. A word flickered
in her mind, then went away.
She yelled at them; they only grew more calm,
more settled in their chairs,
their eyes more firmly fixed on hers.

It was like trying to outstare the cat.
She turned away, confused. Picked up her suitcase.
There must be somewhere she could go.
But no one would tell her, and somehow
she lost the suitcase and somehow
she ended up here, on a sidewalk
on the other side of town. The setting sun
shines straight in her eyes, and she can't tell
if that bus she hears is coming or going.

None of this matters, not even the strangers
with their coffee and talk; nothing matters
except what was written on the door.
She can't stop thinking of her name
on the door, and below it the words
she could not untangle.

The road

Catherine, under the old pine again,
dreams herself riding down a gravel road.
The houses stand back beyond the fields;
there's no one to tell her where this road leads.
Catherine leans on the handlebars, pedalling hard.

When she turns at a crossroad
and stops to rest, a forest surrounds her.
The road is a narrow track
springy with pine needles.
An old road that could show her things,
perhaps a lake beyond the trees.
Already Catherine thinks she sees it:
a flash of reflected sunlight far off.

But here the houses stand close by,
it's dinner time, and she's invited in.
Catherine can't wait. She begs a sandwich
for her pocket, snatches up the bike.
She has to find that lake, that flash
of mirrored light, before light fades.
The people call her from their doorways.
She won't hear.

How to remember

Catherine has a small wooden horse.
Brown and sturdy, it stands
head high, feet poised, intelligent and ready.
Legs, hooves, hindquarters, slope of shoulder
neatly formed; deft brushwork
defines the face, the mane and tail.
Her great-grandfather made it.
His favourite horse, fixed in memory
by knife-strokes, brush and paint.
She takes the carved figure from the shelf,
runs a finger down its neck, along its back,
touches the points of its ears.
She has no picture of the old man himself,
but in her dreams he has a long face
and loves the smell of the grass.

What slips away

Catherine is counting snowflakes,
standing with face tilted
into the spinning flurry of white.
They kiss her upturned lips,
prickle her nostrils, blink in her eyes.
Catherine counts by twos,
by fours, faster
and faster, until she stumbles.
Laughing, gasping, she calls out,
Stop, stop, I lost count!
Snow clings to her hair.
She waits, slowly walks, then runs,
stretching arms out to catch every flake—
every point of delicate geometry—
trips over absurdity, runs again.

What remains

Catherine, far from home, sits under a tree
writing postcards with coloured pens:
blue, orange, lime green. At the post office,
under cobwebbed chandeliers, she will press
a moistened stamp to each card.
She will mail them to herself, to her aunts,
to all those who will ask
How was your trip?
—to whom she will answer: *It was nice.*

Weeks, months later, the postcards will arrive,
and she'll think she is reading someone else's words.
Her aunts will read them like pages from a book
found in the back of a second-hand shop,
one of those nineteenth-century accounts
of the pyramids or Angkor Wat.

Catherine writes as fast as she can
so that, years from now, she can say
*Yes, it was wonderful. To see so much
that was new. Here,
let me show you.*

At the edge of sight

Catherine in a large restaurant
sips fruit punch on ice,
ignores the waiters brushing past her elbows,
and tries to steer the conversation
in a safer direction because
she now sees what is waiting
behind her companion's shoulder.

She has felt like this before:
felt this prickle of anticipation
watching snow fall in the afternoons,
certain that something was waiting
just behind that screen of white
and if she could just shift her eyes
the right way, she would see it.

But it might be unwise to say this.
Presumptuous, anyway, to think
she can tell the shape of another's shadow.

What do you keep looking at?
her companion finally asks,
turning around. *What do you see*
back there?

Coming back

Catherine finds the building easily.
It's empty-looking, tall and narrow.
She climbs the stairs
from the dim ground floor upward
into sunlight: stairs upon stairs,
and on each level a single closed door.
Finally, the top. She pushes the white door
gently, and hears a radio inside
and quiet voices, unfamiliar
as her own voice on a recording.

She catches a word here and there,
a fragment of song, then her name,
and without thinking, she knows
how badly she wants to go in,
how many things she will tell
the ones inside, how much
they already know.

But Catherine will go no farther.
She pulls the door shut,
turns away, skims down the stairs
and stands, heart pounding,
once more at the bottom. Relieved

yet still uneasy, because of the white walls
and the door, the music from the radio;
because she almost went inside.

This stone, and this

who is it you hear speak as you speak sing as you sing what voices live in you?

—Patrick Friesen

Eigenheim

This August day of wind, heat.
Dust from cars' arrival.
This white wooden church, these
steps to twin front doors.
These handshakes, this embrace and kiss
of aunts from far away. This hymn,
my voice faltering on the refrain.
    And after,
this path from front steps to graveyard,
these hands holding, this roar
of passing pickup on the highway,
these strawberry leaves among the stones.
This raw earth enclosing my uncle's body.
Our family's name on this stone, and this.

J.J.

Each picture has its thousand words,
its memoir, map, recording; its home movie
played on Grandpa's own antique projector.
Each grainy newsprint photo sparks remembrance:
Last winter's bowling team. Main Street, 1909.
Obituaries, cut off after photo, name, and date.
Threshing crews lined up in front of
their great iron horses.
                              That scene repeated
on soft scrapbook pages, rewinding time:
Steam-hiss of cylinders, dried-grass smell of chaff.
Muscle memory, swing-rhythm of pitching wheat
from wagon to thresher's mouth.
The dawn-to-dusk momentum of men,
pitchforks, belt and flywheel, straw and grain.

(His voice remembered, his tapping finger
on the page. But I've never tossed a sheaf
or stoked a boiler. I don't know the words
the men called to each other in early morning,
at dinner time, at day's end.)

Dora

She rolled and cut cookies,
sandwiched them with jam,
spread them with marshmallow topping,
sprinkled them with coconut.
She baked a white cake with walnuts,
covered the layers with icing.
She poured cream on her salad.

Those boys are good eaters, she said,
about the cousins from Alberta.
Don't you want dessert? she asked
my mother, every time.

It's more than I'm willing to do,
all the rolling, cutting, spreading
for a few bites of sweetness. But still,
this day in May, with peonies in full
extravagant bloom, a trick of mind
turns their pink and white
to marshmallow and coconut
and I'm in her kitchen again,
fresh cookies on the table.

Is your apartment warm? she asks.
Do you have a new dress for summer?
Are you getting enough to eat?

H.T.

All his children are here. They surround
the open grave and consider what they knew
of him. How he rarely smiled.

Was kann es Schön'res geben
und was kann sel'ger sein...
Their voices rise and fall into
the slow swing of the hymn.

Shovels pass hand to hand.
Hard earth rings on the coffin lid.
Pastor, father, farmer: he had
no more selves than most.
Yet in stories exchanged, overheard,
there's always something you never knew.

...Als wenn wir unser Leben
dem Herrn im Glauben weih'n.
A strong wind hurtles through the graveyard.
The melody climbs,
falls to rest.

Elisabeth

1.
The next day
we walk into her room, and stare
at the neatly made bed, desk,
hand-painted cookie tin, and on the wall
the *Neukirchener Kalender*
with a scripture text for each day.
Well, Mom says finally, *I guess*
this won't bring her back.
And suddenly I want to take things.

2.

Tucked in my dresser drawer, the tiny tea set:
oval tray that fits in my palm, teapot
that doesn't pour, creamer, sugar bowl,
one flowered cup. Her gift on my ninth birthday.
At the party, she talked to my friends
with an ease I learned to admire.
She knew what mattered and what didn't.
She could bend without breaking.

3.
We sat in her front porch, working
with needle and yarn on a toeless sock.
She learned sewing and mending
at school, she said, and showed me
how to reinforce a worn-out heel.

It takes a lot of love. And a lot of firmness,
she said, about raising children. That was all.

How did you do it all? I would ask now.
Did you catch yourself shouting sometimes?

And what—I want to ask,
mending sweaters with the stitch
she taught me—does love look like
on winter afternoons when the washing's
not done and there's all the family
to feed?

4.
She lived, as a child, on the Island of Chortitza
        in the Dniepr River.
She was the eldest of six, the last to marry.
She came to live at Eigenheim near Rosthern.
She married a widower with nine children.
She bore eight children herself.
She never cut her hair short.
She enjoyed Chinese Checkers.
She never spoiled her grandchildren.
She had messy handwriting.
She spoke good English.
She encouraged her children to read.
She kept a diary.

5.
A friend asked if I'd found her again.
No, I said, *only the empty place*
where she used to be. But that night I saw her
in a dream, walking through a wide room
like the kitchen in a church basement
with the same erect bearing, the same grace,
unnoticed by the other women, busy
making coffee, slicing buns, counting pies—
she walked through. That was all.

Photo, 1928

A boy in a little chair
on a wooden verandah,
toy guitar in his lap.
He slouches, face crumpled.
A stout woman beside him,
hand on his forehead,
turns to someone out of frame,
calling, anxious.

But it didn't happen like this,
a sunny day and the boy in short pants.
No, it would have been at night:
the sudden, barking cough, then
breath whistling through swollen windpipe.

No one ever said to me
This is Norman, the day
he got so sick, and this
is Aunt Agatha beside him.
I just knew. And now I don't.
A memory of a lost photograph
isn't much to go on.

This much is true: there was an Aunt Agatha,
dark-haired and stout. There was a boy
who should have been my uncle.
There is a grave.
My grandfather showed me.

Angle of reflection

An amateur's new camera,
jokes to get them laughing.
Black box held steady for the shutter click,
an instant clipped from a summer afternoon.
Who are they? I ask.

They're in a field, row of trees behind them.
Skirts to their ankles, white blouses.
And the young men—shirtsleeves, suspenders,
hats perched high on their heads.
Easy to mistake their age.

That one looking down, sun in her eyes—
That's Judith, Grandpa's first wife, says my mother.
This one's hand smothers a giggle—
and that's your grandma there.

And then the figures lift a little, become
stereoscopic by some mixture
of daylight through yellow curtains,
my mother's voice reciting names,
my eyes' new skill at shifting focus.

If they could stay like this, so young,
ready to step off the Kodak paper—
Are there more? I ask.

The known world

What have I become? The house would know.

—Barbara Nickel

The house on 10th Street

It was large then, a library
of openings and closings, doors
and drawers. I moved across tracts
of linoleum on hands and knees
toward spaces my small arms could span.
The dining table was roof and walls,
was *in, under, through.*
Sewing machine in spindly-legged cabinet
was a swing-open door, was blue and green
of thread, spool clacking on spool
stacked on wooden pegs.
Bookshelves a crackle of dust covers
under my splayed hands.
And the kitchen cupboard with
the turning shelf that moved
each time I pushed it,
that one was *around*
and *around again.*

Taking turns

He's the farmer chasing me.
I'm the horse running away,
front porch to back, around
the rectangle of our house.
I tell him I'm in disguise—glasses,
floppy hat. *Yeah, I saw the horse.*
He went that way.
I can trick the farmer so easy,
twice in a row. The third time
he catches me.

Then I'm a man with a new TV.
He's a thief, grabbing the set
from my living room.
I chase him, back porch to front.
He fools me twice.
Guy with a TV? he says.
Over there—he points,
and I tear around the corner
of the house. But the third time
I catch him.

Table graces

Mornings while we dress
water bubbles in the kettle,
news and weather murmur
from the kitchen radio.
Reading and prayers, each
of us in turn. My brother ends
with *Come dear Lord*
and be our guest. Then
corn flakes with milk, small glass
of juice, toast with gooseberry jam.
Or bran flakes in the bowl,
rhubarb jam on the toast.

We come home at noon to brown buns
with salami, a little lettuce, maybe cheese.
Canned fruit and cookies after.
It's *Come dear Lord* quickly mumbled, then
a retreat into separate worlds—
the Old West, the Future, Middle Earth—
until the afternoon's intrusion.

For supper, a steaming casserole,
dill pickles, bread and butter.
Dessert every night. We're fond of sweets.
My brother begins: *and let this food*
to us be blessed. Amen. We joke,
argue, fall silent. We remark on
the state of the world.
We pass the milk.

Summer at the pool

The change room was small and smelled
of chlorine and wet clothes. It didn't matter
that we were all girls in there, we undressed
under towels, facing the wall.
The big girls weren't as modest. So
we looked sometimes—slipped our eyes sideways,
watched them crook their arms behind their backs
to fasten tiny hooks.

They were distant from us now—fourteen,
too old to comprehend. At ten
I could still feel time revolve in place.
I moved from the change room
into sun-splashed water, and back.
School followed summer followed school.
It would be like this forever.

Incident in August

1.
In the town's biggest church neighbours sit,
quiet. Still raw from the news.

Girls from school gather in the balcony,
a choir in navy and white.
Sunlight sits heavy on our shoulders.
My friend from next door thinks
she's going to faint. I worry,
wonder if I might faint too,
what it would feel like.
Children of the heavenly Father we sing.
For this dear little girl says the priest.
Then it's over.

2.
Two weeks before: I know
which girl they're talking about.
Dark complexion, long hair shading her face,
wide mouth turned up at the corners.
A bit chubby, the women say.

She and I talked once, in the deep end,
elbows propped on the lip of the pool.
I'm still a dog-paddler, but she
was a dolphin in white and blue.

Now she's held in everyone's mind,
balanced on an edge, poised
to be caught or to fall.

3.
Hot days with no news.
Her father in the grocery store,
hands shaking, begins to shout
You've got to do something!

Police search alleys, the schoolyard,
culverts under the tracks.
Then out of town, into the ditches.

Rain clouds loom and pass over.
All anyone wants is to know,
one way or the other.

4.
Afterwards, cucumbers need picking.
Kids feel August stretching out.
People name names, say the guy got off easy.
Cycling out of town, my mother passes
the place where they found her. It's a week
till school starts. I go back to the pool.

Instruction

In 5C on the second floor it was the year
of *Lost in the Barrens* and *Tom Sawyer,*
of lines on maps: Shield, Lowland,
Cordillera marked in coloured pencil.
We drew rivers joining and parting,
veins and arteries exchanging fluid,
the six phases of mitosis,
the journeys of Radisson and La Salle.

In the basement the girls watched films
that explained what we halfway knew,
that gave cheerful advice on hygiene
but didn't mention blood. At home
we read booklets that named
and diagrammed what was in us,
about to begin. Wanting and not wanting
this attention to our changing selves,
here at the edge of the known world.

Tales from Grandma's house

In the brown cupboard in the spare room
in the house by the post office lived Sleeping Beauty
and the boy who would be king
on slips of coloured celluloid that glowed
in the window-light through Viewmaster lenses.
Princess Aurora like a glass figurine,
young Arthur taking the sword from the stone,
enacting the fate set out for them
in seven stereoscopic views.

On the next shelf lived Struwwelpeter,
wild hair and curling fingernails menacing
from the front cover. His stories
all cautionary tales: Eat your soup.
Don't play with matches. Don't suck
your thumb. No knowledge of German
needed, the Or Else obvious
in the bright flames devouring the girl's dress,
her cats weeping over her ashes. Long-legged
Scissors Man lopping off thumbs.
The fussy eater dwindling to a stick,
a soup tureen for a headstone.
Children, says Struwwelpeter,
here's a destiny you can change.

Shy

Age five: mother and aunt conclude
I'll never say it. They write on cardboard,
tie my Red Riding Hood cape,
nudge me toward neighbours' doors
with the sign around my neck: *Trick or Treat.*

*

Grade four: girls in the washroom
fill the cramped passage from doorway to stalls
with hair-brushing and gossip.
A few mumbled words (*'scuse me,
c'n I get through*) and they
would shift aside without a look.
But tongue-tied, itching to slip by
wordless, I must wait to be noticed.

*

Grade nine, a list of things
impossible to say:
Actually, my name's not Joan.
That wasn't fair.
Hello, can I speak to—?
Yeah, so? You're ugly too.

Fifteen

Sometimes I wonder what would happen
if I screamed at someone. It's like
I'm scared to get angry, like if I do
my insides will melt or something.
Or no one will talk to me again.

She lies in bed, wide-eyed,
ears grasping for any sound,
any tiny hint that her fears are coming to life
(as the clothes on the chair used to do,
growing large and threatening after dark).

I dreamed about fire, and in the dream
I woke up and the bed was burning.
There were voices in the flames telling me
to come, but when I stepped
out of bed I fell through the floor.
When I woke up
I could still hear those voices.

Her mother only said: "Go to sleep.
Nothing's going to happen." Still,
she checked the stove twice
before crawling into bed.

I answered the altar call again
and still don't feel any different.
You're supposed to feel different, they said,
you should have peace in your heart. I don't know
what's supposed to happen next.
I don't want to go to hell.

Now she lies plotting her escape
so that she will not be engulfed
when flames creep up the stairs.

July

Do you remember how warm the nights were,
how we ended the days dog-tired,
drunk with fresh air?
We imagined things by firelight
that daylight wouldn't permit.
Or maybe that was just me.

You paid no special attention to me.
I was never alone with you. Still—
there was that one night. It was late,
I guess. Only three of us still up.
I don't know what you meant to do,
but your casual touch in the dark
brought distant things suddenly close—
brought a warm rush of desire
before I knew what that was.

Of course I was silly.
Of course I blame you.
Don't you know what you did?
I was so sure I loved you.

Wu's Café

Dinner For Four, with agreed-upon favourites—
won ton soup, egg rolls, chow mein—
near the end of a day's travel,
four of us trying out adulthood
in a second-hand car. Nine hours
of highway bringing us a new city,
new school, the answers we're looking for,
questions we have yet to ask.

Afterwards we unwrap the folded wafers,
snap them apart. We expect
the usual promises: love, luck,
and fortune. Surprised, then, to find
one slip that doesn't promise anything,
that names, instead, a present need
for courage.

But why not? A random draw
still turns up a useful card.
The fortune cookie, though inedible,
might tell you something almost wise.
Not quite providence, but a word
that echoes an unacknowledged ache.
An accidental message that you keep
just in case it really is for you.

We're in a foreign country

And you, stumbling at the edges of your self

—Jan Zwicky

First night

We're in a foreign country: narrow street, closed-in sky. Outside in the not-quite-dark we watch rain fall in sheets, yellow streetlight reflected off the clouds. It's late August. Today we stepped off a plane, limp from travel, into sticky Ontario heat, and set our suitcases down in hollow rooms. Two weeks till the furniture arrives—couch, wooden desk, the cat's favourite chair. And so in the evening we stand on the porch. Not talking, not yet. Not for days.

Later you tell me how much you want to go back. *There are no good restaurants here*, you say, as if that explains everything. But on the first night we stand near the porch railing, out of the rain, close enough to feel spray on our faces. I'm thinking of home, how it's no longer static, but follows us from place to place. Now it's a suite in an old brick house. Before this an apartment over a flower shop, a house with a purple door. I'm thinking how places forget you after you leave: blinds suddenly hang straighter, rhubarb disappears from the garden. We go inside, lay our sleeping bags on bare floors, fall asleep by an open window. It rains all night.

In the basilica

Blue vaulted ceiling dusted with gold stars. Ranks of votive candles warming the feet of statues. I slip into a front pew and try not to think. There's a woman crouched on the chancel steps, her head against the rail. Young, maybe thirty, with dark, curly hair. She sits very still, her skirt gathered beneath her. She is crying.

She stays there a long time. I begin to think she is an icon. Martha at the grave of Lazarus: *Lord, if you had been here...* The widow before the hard-hearted judge: *Grant me justice.* Or even Jacob wrestling with God: *I will not let you go unless you bless me.*

I should not look at her. She is here to be safe, to weep without having to explain. Yet I can't take my eyes from her. Light from coloured windows transforms her, turns her hair to carved and polished wood. I want to light a candle, place it next to her. I want to burden her with longings I'm hardly aware of. But she stands, finally, and with head erect walks up the centre aisle and out the door.

In the end

she settles for plain cardboard. It seems the best idea, and the thing
has to be put away. People told her she should quit pretending,
face up to it. After some time she decided they were right, and
she put her last, deepest heartache out on the mantelpiece. But
now she can't stand the way it looks at her. She hates touching it
when she dusts on Saturdays. It has to go somewhere else. Up in
the cupboard—but even there it will look at her when she opens
the door. No, a box is best. At first she thinks Plexiglas. Clear and
unbreakable. At least she won't have to touch the thing. But the
children will still ask questions, and won't understand when she
doesn't answer. Maybe a locked chest?—too obvious. No, an old box
from the garage, labelled with felt marker. Put away upstairs with
the other boxes and bags, where she can find it if she really wants
to. And when the children play in the attic, they won't know it from
the rest of the old junk up there.

The rain

has a language of its own, chanting hard and fast as it pounds
the roof. Harder, louder. Now the storm centre is overhead. A
thunderclap shakes the house, and the power goes out. TV and
radio are silent. We drift into the living room, talk about getting
candles. No one goes to find them. I play the piano in the dark. We
all look shadowy, blurred around the edges. The sound of rain fills
the room. Conversation fades, movement stops. I wait for words
to emerge, but there are none, only consonants chattering on the
shingles.

This is like that Sunday last summer when we drove to Martins
Lake, a sudden rain pelting our little green car. Mom said this
was ridiculous, we should turn back and Dad said, well, this was
a driving rain and we were driving in it. The horizon disappeared;
the grid road was a brown smudge. When we emerged, there was
the lake with its gravelly beach and ugly little cabins, everything
shining wet. And a rainbow. But in the middle of it there was
nothing to see, there was only sound. Like now. Sound holds us in
place, it's a struggle even to think. I want to figure out what the rain
is saying, I want to know what my mother is thinking as she stands
at the window. I don't want the rain to end.

On Yonge Street, yesterday

A man smoking a pipe passes you on the sidewalk. You don't notice
him until the trail of smoke catches your nose. You turn and look,

but he's at the corner now, the light's green, he's crossing—is that
him?—you follow his head, shoulders, the slight swing of his arms.
Now he's a small silhouette. Now an indistinct form within the mass
of people moving toward lunchtime cafés

and now you're sure: he wore a grey coat, his scarf was blue.

He smoked a long-stemmed briar.

He looked like someone you know.

Noise

You have to pretend it's all noise—I mean the things people say. *I can't get it ready today, she's crazy... did I tell you what happened last night?... you shoulda seen what we did to his car...* You know how people talk on the street, as if no one else is around, as if it doesn't matter who hears. They forget how words escape, the way pressed flowers fall out of old books when you pick them up. Before you catch them they're blown away, trampled underfoot. Gone—like words spoken in passing, out there for anyone to catch, for the wind to blow in someone's face. It's happened again, this time from a man in a blue overcoat and a woman in fur. *Faith is the substance of things hoped for,* he says. *O ye of little faith,* she answers with a wry smile. Then they're gone, I can't hear any more. I gaze after them, wanting to follow, to demand more than this flippant exchange of phrases. Yet they walk away without slowing their pace. I'm the one left stumbling over what they've said, unable to shift its unexpected weight.

Clues

We sat at a corner table, our faces in shadow, she with a glass
of Chablis and the *Globe and Mail* in front of her. She rubbed
the newsprint, examined the smudge of ink on her finger. *What*
happens, she said, *to all those words? What are they, bullets or rubber*
balls? Do they bounce back, or touch target and explode? Long pause.
Maybe they're stray confetti. Maybe they gather dust in corners. She
stared down at her hands, let her fingers trace paths among the
cutlery. The checkered tablecloth became an empty diagram with
numbered squares. A waiter appeared. *The clues are here,* he said,
handing her the menu. *24-down,* she replied, *and give my friend*
13-across and a piece of advice. He nodded, turned to me: *Try the*
special: 7-across, six letters, first is 's.' He left, and she bent over the
tablecloth, filling in squares.

Through a glass

No one came to take our order. *At least we have wine,* I said. She
poured some for each of us, saying nothing. I looked around and
behind us to catch a waiter glancing our way. At other tables, people
ate salad, then veal, then petit-fours. Then they left, singly and by
twos. The lights dimmed. She didn't seem to mind. She looked out
the window, at me, out the window again. The candle sputtered and
smoked. *Do you think,* I said, and stopped. She rolled the stem of
her wineglass between her fingers. The place was quiet as a closed
book, quiet as liquid pouring into a cup, quiet as rain when you're
not even sure it's raining. Her face was like a windowpane with a
dark sky outside. She looked at me through the Merlot and said:
*You know, this is what God is like. A good wine, the kind you dance
around with adjectives but never quite describe.* It was the only thing
she said all evening. Her face rippled in the candle smoke. She put
down the glass and looked at me. Waited. Just waited.

Holding onto gravity

Down by the water, below the city, a man and woman sit on a rock. The broad river wears sunshine like a new scarf; a gravel path hugs the steep bank. The man and woman make a tight circle, half facing each other, his arm around her.

This is better, the woman thinks. She feels more solid here. Up in the city things have no weight—not the people, not even cars or stone buildings. She has to wear something to hold her down—thick-soled shoes, or in winter a woollen coat. She walks with small steps, eyes flitting left and right. Sometimes in the midst of sorting papers she looks out her sixth-floor office window, over lawn and parking lot and trees, to the building opposite, and a vivid sense of depth and distance overwhelms her. A space opens up inside, like she's filled with air, her bones hollow like a bird's. This feeling frightens her. What if her senses are deceiving her? Or worse, what if they aren't?

She knows all kinds of illusions are possible. But down here nothing makes her fearful, not even the fast water so close by. She presses her palms flat on the rock. Her companion takes a small stone, dips it in the water, places it in her lap.

Quietly but much too near

...all things have had this hair-breadth escape:
everything has been saved from a wreck.

—G.K. Chesterton

No map

We lay beside a spent fire,
far from home, sheltered
in a hollow lined with short grass.
Fringe of poplars obscured
the horizon. Across the river
coyotes howled.

What were we to do? No map,
nothing in our pockets. I stared at the sky,
trying to slow my breath.

You slept soundly and woke late.
A hot morning, the wind just enough
to rattle poplar leaves.
You said, *Are you afraid?*
I looked down, ground my heel
into the grass,
answered *Yes.*

Three o'clock

The maple tree casts a forked shadow
on the lawn under the streetlight.
Each solitary car that passes
leaves jarring echoes in our sleep.
Across the street, the fire in the parked car
is out, firefighters gone.
Neighbours, startled from their beds
by light and noise, have drifted back inside.
They lie restless, thinking of their children.
We, too, rest uneasily. Every creak and rustle
is something crumbling, shattering,
quietly but much too near.

Encircled

Did you hear something?
Yes.

Faint cat-scratch, wanting out
or wanting in. A shadow flits
across the wallpaper. Something
passed the front door. .
Someone outside just spoke.

A trickle in the pipes: water running
in the upstairs suite.
Footsteps on the stairs, or
just the house shifting.
A tree branch scrapes
against the siding.

Did you lock the door?
I think so.

It doesn't take much,
one claw on the screen
and there's a hole.

Stories

We sit on the front porch listening
to bamboo chimes in the wind,
and you talk about the red-haired baby you saw
on the bus today, how it lay in its carriage
staring at you, revolving its little white feet.
It's like she knew something, you say,
and try to laugh. *Knew what?* I say,
and tease you, make wild guesses.
You don't smile.

So I tell you about the night you were away,
the house so quiet I couldn't sleep.
The phone rang after midnight—a man calling
from Hong Kong. *No,* I said, *he doesn't live here.*
Maybe long ago, not now. No. Pushing against
his certainty, I began to doubt what I knew
of you. Wanted you home again,
just to be quite sure.

Pause

In the car on the darkening street
conversation stops. Your silence,
overlaid with mine, grows thick.
I test the weight of words
that might dislodge it,
discard them one by one.
The last one gone, my hands
fall empty to my lap.

And yet—oh, the arrogance of it—
I still want to have your soul
in my keeping, to know
what you yourself don't know

(where have you been?
where are you now?
when will you come back?)

Sitting together, not quite touching

Women are opaque, he said,
leaning back on the sofa after an evening of TV.
She thought it was unfair, the way
he always said these things
on days when she felt most transparent.
Maybe, she thought, the opaqueness was
what he saw when he looked through her.
She asked him, *What are you looking at?*
so that he could answer, *The back of your throat*
where all the words are waiting
till it's safe to come out.
But she knew he would never say this
and felt foolish for hoping.
What are you looking at? he asked.
She looked away, not wanting to answer.
Your hands, she finally said. *They look*
like they belong to someone else.

Railway bridge, 33rd Street

She will fall. She knows this.
One day she will fall from this height,
helpless, and drown in the undertow.
She watches others climb:
walking to work, so casual,
hoping a train will pass
so they can feel the bridge tremble.
Her hands grip tight to the railing.

But she comes here to feel the wind,
to turn small, light, transparent,
and to look down through her panic
at the river ice below,
milky green and crazed
like a mosaic made of glass.
River disappears into sky,
and she wants to follow.
She wants to walk straight
into the horizon.

Babes in the woods

Got to get a trail cleared through here,
he said. *And warn people about poison ivy.*
His boots champed through the undergrowth;
his hatchet snicked off a young branch.

Remember those kids, he said suddenly,
the ones that got lost here a while back?
Kidnapped, people said. Lived off nuts and berries
for a while, and then just died,
no one knows how. I think it was bears.
He had more to say, but I stopped listening.
I was trying to catch an old song
that appeared out of nowhere

> (oh dear do you know
> how a long time ago)

Half the words were missing.
I thought I saw them

> (oh don't you remember)

behind a birch tree, or maybe
under the wild strawberries:
children playing hide-and-seek, flirting,
half wanting to be found—and then
running off, going a little too far.
I stopped. Waited. Called out:
Ready or not, here I come.

Listen

all the tones

melding into curve
and movement—
something I can ride.

—Jean Janzen

Mistrust of language

Finally you were left alone
because the words refused to follow
your headlong rush into the undergrowth,
couldn't find your trail among fallen leaves,
lost sight of you amid flickering shadows.

You were gone for a year and a day.
I saw you when you returned.
You brought no journal, no photographs,
not even a single pressed flower.
You showed me just one thing:
a handful of small stones
you've carried in your pockets
ever since.
              And now you tell me
you will never write again. Instead,
when you go out on these cool fall days
you will finger the stones as you walk,
a wordless chant to the rhythm of your feet.

Snowstorm

Next morning it's knee-deep
on the sidewalks. All traffic vanished,
silence expands to fill its place.
In your basement apartment we make coffee,
burrow in afghans, turn on the radio,
the voice a reassurance. Last night
we watched the city disappear.

Around midday, a new sound: some guy
buzzing a snowmobile down the street
just because he can. The noise grows louder,
retreats. Swells and fades again, a drone
under endless reports of the weather.
Restless, we peer out through drifted windows,
reach for coats.

Outside, clarity has returned.
Each footfall, each breath draws an outline
in still air. The cold sears our throats.
And the empty four-lane street
is a footpath extravagantly wide
for the two of us alone.

Rondo

1.
Around midnight the air finally cools
and people walk slowly in the park.
A man, unseen in the dark pavilion,
plays a banjo and sings.
A passerby hears a sound
(rain on a window, or
dry leaves on pavement)
and turns her head.

2.
On a sky-blue September afternoon it comes
from a shaded front porch. An old man
with a violin, his back to the street.
Letting phrases rise and fall,
letting them go.

3.
Midnight again, high above the river.
We cruise the quiet path on bikes,
you in the lead. I hear it first:
in the willows, a harmonica
plays a tune I can't name.
The player invisible.

Rhapsody no. 2

I like Brahms, says my teacher,
brushing her hair with her fingertips
and lifting her chin a little.
She likes Brahms, so I'm learning it.
I start again, try to make the sound fatter,
the way she wants it.

As I leave I admire her house.
Yes, she says, chin up again, *I've lived here
since before the flood.* I think
of Noah's ark and stifle a laugh.

Days later I learn about the flood
in the fifties. I wonder, how far
did the water come? Did it fill this street,
come up the front step, slip under the door?
I practise amid visions of my teacher
playing Brahms underwater on that same piano.
That's why she keeps saying *bigger;*
the heavy sound reminds her of
the waterlogged keys, dripping books,

the weight of her feet in rubber boots.
Her last adventure before a long
unromantic career prodding students
toward exams and recitals. Oh, but in the flood
she was heroic. She waded through the streets
and heaved sandbags with the best of them.

Well, she says next time,
with the merest hint of satisfaction,
that's better.

Suite Française
by Francis Poulenc

It's a good day for dissonance.
Playing the piano with all the windows open,
barefoot, in an old cotton dress.
Wind flings the curtain at my neck,
bringing in the scent of rain.
Slowly first. Fingers recall the pattern:
stretched past the octave, then tangled
in clashing chords. Again and again,
the stamping rhythm. In tempo now,
no looking down, let my hands leap.
Make the lightning come closer.
I'm running downhill too fast,
wind shoving at my back,
can't stop and think or I'll fall.
Rain comes in the window and I play
till thunder startles me witless
and I sit still, panting,
letting the storm take over.

Fugue on the Magnificat

Pachelbel and rain, dim light
on organ keys. Shadows
in the rafters, ribs
of an upside-down ship
parting the water. Down the panes
of pebbled glass, drip by drop,
eighth notes in steady quick-step.
I'm practising someone else's prayers,
a means to sharpen my own longing
for that constant love to which
each phrase of counterpoint gives answer.
Rain crescendos to fullness, a deep *Amen*
on pedal notes that re-echo in the woodwork.
I hold the last long chord, close the book.
Tomorrow I'll return, repeat
and repeat the task.
Each progress a beginning.

Theme and Variations

After Beethoven's Piano Sonata no. 30 in E major

It's dark, late evening.
Light wind through the elms.
The air smells like rain.

1.
That windy evening in the park.
Why don't we climb? you said.
We sat on a branch, low in the massive pine
and lost count of the times we kissed.

2.
Talk to me, I said
at the end of a long, hot day.
We sat on the balcony, waited
for any small movement of air.

3.
Two a.m. and you weren't there
beside me in the dark bed.
You were somewhere on a roadside
waiting out the blinding rain.
I lay awake, imagined calamities.

4.
Almost dark. We walked home
from the café in the rain. I said
because I love you, but couldn't explain
how that answered your question.

5.
We brought home chicken for dinner,
spread a tablecloth, filled glasses.
Drank to discovery, the surprise of each other.
Lit candles and turned out the lights.

6.
Late evening, it's dark.
You at your desk. I pass
behind you, pause
to touch your hair.
There's a light wind in the elms.
The air smells like rain.

Listen

At this early hour you can sit
undisturbed in the kitchen.
At this hour it's so quiet
you can hear clocks ticking upstairs,
the baby crying next door,
a promise of love whispered
in the next city. So quiet
you can hear the continents drifting,
your own cells breathing.

When it's quiet like this, so early,
you and I can whisper stories
so softly that only the cats can hear—
though maybe the others, still sleeping,
will turn and mutter as if they heard us.
Perhaps we are telling their dreams;
perhaps they are dreaming our stories.
How far can a whisper carry?
How soft must our voices be
to reach across the ocean?

Evensong

Good shepherd and sheep glowing red,
jewel colours in east windows stained
by the flare of revolving lights.
Low voices, a shuffle behind back pews,
blue uniforms bend over a woman on the floor.
The huddled watchers defer, giving room
to the skilled, poised to fetch water,
clasp a hand, whatever's asked.
Attendants murmur: *Can you hear me?*
Can you speak? Along the nave
the bent heads in rows, the call
and response: *Hear us. Deliver us.*

Things I can't get rid of

And in some language
there must be a word for this distance, find it and write it over and
over

—Sue Goyette

Torn apart

1.
They're tearing the old sanatorium down.
Behind barricades and No Trespassing signs
men in hard hats stroll through the grounds.
Radiators lie piled up on the lawn;
brick comes off the frame bit by bit.

2.
That big house down the street
with the sagging porch and green roof,
bulldozed in a morning.
By noon it lay in splinters.

3.
That quiet black-haired boy—
how, sudden and unexplained,
he tore body and soul apart
with a slender noose of rope.

The lost one

The dreams told her something had happened.
Some nights she heard her mother talk
about the time before her birth:
We were so close, you and I, and then
when you were born something was gone—
and when she woke all that remained
was the one word *gone*.

Other nights it was different:
an old friend, a lover disappearing
silently around a corner.
Her house, emptied. Walls blank,
closets bare.
In the dreams she wrote words with missing letters,
said *full* and heard *empty*.
In the dreams she could never say *child*.

In the kitchen, afternoon

Two friends sit together. The room is still
except for the chink of cup on saucer.
One tells how she almost had a child, once.
How it disappeared before it could be seen;
how aftermath of pain left her dumb.
It was hardly a child, she says.
It was still just a dream, a secret.

The other is silent. She wants to say:
a death is a death.
She wants to ask:
what did you name this dream?

Thaw

You have to take your chances as they come.
Two days ago, finally a thaw
and the dry snow turned sticky.
Outside, quickly: roll one ball, then another—
sweating with the weight of it—
third ball on top, bottle caps for the face,
and done. Just in time: today the head tilts,
body slumps toward earth.

If it were always this easy to do
what the time demands.
Chances get missed, questions linger:
why did you swallow those pills?
what did you really want?

You gave me the chance to ask.
That weekend in spring, lounging
in your old armchairs, exchanging news.
We'd been roommates, travel-mates, shared
an affinity for butter tarts and music—and still
some words would not push past my tongue.

Not pills in the end, but cancer.
Nothing could have changed that.
Nothing to do now but rebel
against your going, the ache of memory,
all the impossible questions.

Blue napkins

Later, over tea, they ask
how I'm doing. And they mean it.
They want to know what it was like
finding out the reprieve was over,
the tumour had hold of you again
and would not let go.
I look down at the cobalt-blue napkins
that remind me of you, as everything does.
How to explain the strangeness of these few days,
being swept away, not sure if I was being lifted high
or dropped. Not sure if this new emptiness
would leave me lighter or weigh me down.
Sure only of this tightness in the chest,
this ache beneath the ribs.

I'm all right, I say. I fold the napkin,
slip it in my pocket,
out of sight.

Afterwards

And now I have things I can't get rid of:

the bookmark you slipped in my mailbox,
message pencilled on the back, signed
with a flourish on the B—

the photo of you on the summer trail
by the river, the tilt of your head,
your over-shoulder grin—

the road trip south in your smoke-blue Chevy,
windows open to the hot breeze,
pronghorns' white rumps receding across a field—

your advice, delivered without preamble:
Look for another job.
It's your wedding, you choose the colour—

the way, at twenty-five, we shook our heads
over our naiveté at twenty.

But the job you had that summer has disappeared.
The music you played—that's missing, too.
And for all my looking I can't find, anywhere,
the last thing you said.

Queen's Park, October

In this corner under the sun, a fountain
ringed with ornamental grasses, tall and tasselled,
a woman under a long-needled pine
doing t'ai chi, all in brown.
A mother and child
watch the wind riffle the water.

Young men in bright nylon jog past,
a cluster of primary colours.
One ducks his head
as a flock of pigeons skims low.

I'm here wanting only clear light,
a stiff wind to revive me. Tired,
ill-equipped to fend off
a rush of remembrance. Your absence.

The woman in brown takes a step
back, her hands pushing forward.
The air around her dances.

Wind sends spray over all of us
clustered around the fountain,
dampening sound, blunting the edges
of memory.

Words from one who has not been there

I tried to tell you the power of that place.
I tried to tell you the sun would burn—

you with your pale skin, pale blue eyes; you,
so enthralled by your discovery of warmth,
eager to go out and spend a day
absorbing bright warm yellow—

but I couldn't tell you. It seemed
the wrong thing to say, especially that day,
with you looking so happy
remembering your summer in Greece,
your skin bright as sunlight, translucent.

You never came back to tell me what happened.
I thought the heat and drought had killed you,

but they said you were all right, you didn't burn.
They said you dissolved into light.

Desire and distance

*Only empty
things fill up again. Now you're ready.*

—Chandra Mayor

In search

I never told the neighbours why
I spent so much time in their gardens
digging through snow, or why
I combed through back alleys in the dark
of early morning.
I tried going in when they invited,
tried to accept their gifts
of homemade bread and jam,
but couldn't. Until finally
I knew what I wanted—something
that can't be caught or enclosed,
that touches what can't be touched,
that seeps through skin.

This is why I can never stay at home.
The wanting builds up, and only a scent
can speak to it.
I walk the February streets
in search of lilacs.

One purple, one white

Up on the roof I can smell blossoms
and feel the cool breeze
that never enters my room.
Two lilac bushes, one purple, one white,
and the garden spread out below
and neighbours' yards, all down the alley.
Then poplar trees, fields, and sky
wide open. Infinite space
tugging at earth-bound objects.

Unnerving for the ones who built
this house a century ago—the way
land and sky erased them,
swallowed them whole. Even here
on the sun-warm shingles,
sheltered from wind, the world is too large.
I'm afraid to move or look over
the edge, but still—how easy
to breathe up here.

Expected

Someone is coming soon. She's pressing
toward arrival and I'm heavy
with waiting, my body slowed,
thinking of her. All I have
is an echo of her, small impacts of limbs
that kick me awake these nights.
I lie restless, toss out curled-up names,
wonder if there's one she will keep
when she unfolds into the world.
I'm losing the need for words,
the power to find them. Soon
all I will know is her intelligence
of flesh and bone and sucking mouth.
We'll speak through skin
touching skin: lips, hands,
my full, aching breasts.

Desire and distance

These keen, unfocused longings come
late in the day, when the lowering sun's rays
streak through the clouds, gathering
the horizon in their stream.
They have a curious way
of making distant towns look like paradise.
I'm going to follow them around the world,
hoping some day to find myself
caught in their sweep.
I'll pursue heaven around the earth,
always looking ahead to the next town—
the one that's glowing gold, the one
where the last orange rays
set every windowpane on fire.
I'm chasing a glimpse of God
that's always farther down the road.
Foolish, maybe, but the choices
were clear: to stay home, watch sunsets,
and paint my longings in watercolours,
or to follow the sun's oblique rays
as if they were Jacob's ladder
and I could find the place
where they touched down.

Nothing to lose

Or suppose a woman has ten silver coins...
                                        —*Luke 15:8*

I spend time these days riding buses.
Not thinking, not speaking,
leaving the world to itself.
Listening to conversations in the seat behind.

A woman's voice. A woman's hand
grasping the seat back near my shoulder.

What saddens me is this, she says: *I found
the silver coin I had lost—swept every corner,
turned out every pocket, finally found it—
but it's no use telling my neighbours. They think
they have no silver coins to lose. They will not,*
she whispers, *they will not open their fists.*

I sit up with a jerk, ring for the next stop,
stumble off, plunge through snow in the park.
Hoarfrost sprinkles down from a tree. Then nothing,
only my own ragged breathing, and the wind
tugging at my hands.

Sometimes this highway

It's hard to get across, some days.
You want to forget the coffee shop
on the other side, you want
to let your feet follow the highway
as far as they can,
anywhere, out of here.

You reach the café by force of will,
order your coffee,
sit far from the window,
keep one eye on the clock.

But you still take note
when the Greyhound passes through.
A five-minute stop, then west
to Saskatoon, North Battleford, Edmonton.

Is no one else tempted
like this? and why
is this landscape so flat
unless to lure you outward
to where the road disappears?

When you return to work
you look both ways before crossing.

Small bones

My brother said he could hear them
outside the bedroom window
crying and crying to get in. He worried.
He thought no one else knew of them
and feared they might die.

He was sure he would find them one day,
their small bones protruding, their noses
stretched forward, sniffing for the bits of cake
we weren't allowed to feed them.
Our mother told us there was nothing out there,
she told us not to be scared,

and we weren't. We longed for wild things.
We drew stories from bent flower stalks,
rushed out after storms to see
what the wind teased out of the treetops.
My brother strode through wet grass,
heedless of cold feet, and I followed,
stepping more gingerly. Wanting so much
for our mother to be wrong just this once.

Barefoot at midnight

On this sleepless night I follow you
down an almost-forgotten road, finally knowing
what keeps you away from home.
Just this: you have learned the value
of discontent. You live between the lines.
You like the way sunlight shifts,
planes separate, spaces open
and some ancient music, faint but insistent,
cuts the air with desire.

You are accustomed to its pull on your body,
the way it tugs your fingers, tightens your throat.
You don't even mind when it comes at night
like this, and draws you from your bed
to travel down this arrow-straight highway.
You're heading north this time,
between sunset and moonrise,
holding the light on either hand.
Running with arms flung wide,
barefoot in the dark.

On the North Saskatchewan, 1981

We reached the bank just in time,
stowed the canoes, took shelter
as clouds churned overhead.
Thunder cracked the sky
and the first hot day,
the first real summer day,
ended in a burst of rain.

Next day another storm,
this one far away, hair-thin lightning
above the horizon, silent, never coming
close enough to threaten.
We watched, admiring, as if
we'd never seen lightning before.

We emerged from that summer knowing
we had changed. We learned
to walk without a flashlight after dark,
to speak without a script.

When the auroras were out we sprawled
on the ground, watched them arch
and flow overhead, then danced
until we fell down again.
Not close enough to wilderness
to feel its danger, young enough
to take the warm night as a gift,
we lay in the grass, ready to slip out
of our skins.

Dreaming red lilies

Remember how we argued about dreams—
whether they were prophecy or foreshadowing;
whether they were anything at all.

Well, what about this, I said: what if I had
a dream of wild prairie lilies—no common thing
these days—and saw them where they grew years ago,
by the path going down to the river.

(A signpost made of flames, you said. I smiled.)

Remember that day when someone picked them all
before anyone could warn her? They never came back.
This dream can't be anything but a flicker of memory,
a snapshot turned over by chance.

Or think of it, you said (almost carelessly),
as a small resurrection.

But if it is, to whom should we tell it,
and how should its gospel be written?

With a blade of grass, you say, on the palm of a hand
so that the blood beneath the skin turns to fire.

Notes on the poems

Eigenheim is the name of a rural community just west of Rosthern, Saskatchewan, and of the Mennonite church located there.

In "J.J." the phrase "rewinding time" is borrowed from a poem of the same name by Sarah Klassen, from her collection *A Curious Beatitude* (The Muses' Company, 2006).

The verse from the German hymn by Karl Johann Philipp Spitta quoted in "H.T." translates roughly as follows: "What can be more beautiful, and what can be more blessed, than when we dedicate our life in faith to the Lord."

"Children of the Heavenly Father," the hymn mentioned in "Incident in August," is by Caroline V.S. Berg, translated by Ernst W. Olson.

Scripture quotations in "In the basilica" are from John 11:32, Luke 18:3, and Genesis 32:26. Quotations in "Noise" are from Hebrews 11:1 and Matthew 16:8 (King James Version). All Scripture quotations, unless otherwise indicated, are taken from the Holy Bible, New International Version®, NIV®. Copyright ©1973, 1978, 1984, 2011 by Biblica, Inc.™ Used by permission of Zondervan. All rights reserved worldwide. www.zondervan.com The "NIV" and "New International Version" are trademarks registered in the United States Patent and Trademark Office by Biblica, Inc.™

The indented lines in "Babes in the woods" are from an Appalachian folk song of the same name.

"Rondo" takes its title from a musical form in which the recurring main theme alternates with contrasting elements.

The epigraph on page ix is from *The Days of our Years: A History of the Eigenheim Mennonite Church Community: 1892-1992* by

Acknowledgments

Some poems in this book, or earlier versions of them, appeared in the following journals: *The Antigonish Review, Bywords, CV2, Carleton Arts Review, Curio Poetry, DRUm/ à bâtons rompus, Fireweed, Graffito, Hook & Ladder, Hostbox, Ink Magazine, The Light Ekphrastic, Other Voices, Pottersfield Portfolio, Pouèt-cafée,* and *Rhubarb.*

My thanks to Laura Lush, Laurie Block and Sarah Klassen, who read the book in its early stages and gave me fresh ways of seeing these poems. Many thanks to Alice Major for her wonderfully insightful editing. I'm grateful for the mentorship program of the Manitoba Writers' Guild, which enabled me to work with Laurie Block. I'm also grateful for the opportunity to work in pleasant and welcoming places: Joel Reimer and Teresa van dan Boogard's home, Kurt and Erika Armstrong's spare room, Ian and Angela Peterson's cottage, St. Benedict's Monastery, and Artscape Gibraltar Point. My thanks to the members of the writers' groups I've been a part of in Ottawa, Toronto and Winnipeg, and to Sally Ito and Angeline Schellenberg for their friendship, support and advice. And to my husband and sons, for being loyal fans and for being their inimitable selves.